Federal Interagency Forum on Child and Family Statistics

America's Children in Brief: Key National Indicators of Well-Being, 2010

This year's America's Children in Brief: Key National Indicators of Well-Being *report continues more than a decade of dedication and collaboration by agencies across the Federal Government to advance our understanding of our Nation's children and what may be needed to bring them a better tomorrow. We hope you find this report useful. The Forum will be releasing its next full report in 2011.*

Katherine K. Wallman, Chief Statistician, Office of Management and Budget

Introduction

Each year since 1997, the Federal Interagency Forum on Child and Family Statistics has published a report on the well-being of children and families. Pending data availability, the Forum updates all 40 indicators annually on its Web site (http://childstats.gov) and alternates publishing a detailed report, *America's Children: Key National Indicators of Well-Being*, with a summary version that highlights selected indicators. The *America's Children* series makes Federal data on children and families available in a nontechnical, easy-to-use format in order to stimulate discussion among data providers, policymakers, and the public.

The Forum fosters coordination and integration among 22 Federal agencies that produce or use statistical data on children and families and seeks to improve Federal data on children and families. The *America's Children* series provides accessible compendiums of indicators drawn across topics from the most reliable official statistics; it is designed to complement other more specialized, technical, or comprehensive reports produced by various Forum agencies.

The indicators and demographic background measures presented in *America's Children in Brief* all have been presented in previous Forum reports. Indicators are chosen because they are easy to understand, are based on substantial research connecting them to child well-being, cut across important areas of children's lives, are measured regularly so that they can be updated and show trends over time, and represent large segments of the population, rather than one particular group.

These child well-being indicators span seven domains: *Family and Social Environment, Economic Circumstances, Health Care, Physical Environment and Safety, Behavior, Education,* and *Health.* This year's report reveals that health insurance coverage rates for children increased, the percentage of preterm births declined for the second straight year, average 8th-grade mathematics scores reached an all-time high, teen smoking was at its lowest since data collection began, and the adolescent birth rate declined after a 2-year increase. However, the percentage of children whose parents had secure employment was the lowest since 1996, and the percentage living in poverty was the highest since 1998. The percentage of children in food-insecure households was the highest since monitoring began. The *Brief* concludes with a summary table displaying recent changes in all 40 indicators.

For Further Information

The Forum's Web site (http://childstats.gov) provides additional information, including:

- Detailed data, including trend data, for indicators discussed in this *Brief* as well as other *America's Children* indicators not discussed here.

- Data source descriptions and contact information.

- *America's Children* reports from 1997 to the present and other Forum reports.

- Links to Forum agencies, their online data tools, and various international data sources.

- Forum news and information on the Forum's overall structure and organization.

Demographic Background

Understanding the changing demographic characteristics of America's children is critical for shaping social programs and policies. The number of children determines the demand for schools, health care, and other services that are essential to meet the daily needs of families. Although the number of children living in the United States has grown, the ratio of children to adults has decreased. At the same time, the racial and ethnic composition of the Nation's children continues to change.

In 2009, there were 74.5 million children in the United States, 2 million more than in 2000. This number is projected to increase to 101.6 million by 2050. In 2009, there were similar numbers of children in each of three age groups: 0–5 years (25.5 million), 6–11 years (24.3 million), and 12–17 years (24.8 million).

Since the mid-1960s, children have been decreasing as a proportion of the total U.S. population. In 2009, children made up 24 percent of the population, down from a peak of 36 percent at the end of the "baby boom" (1964). Children are projected to remain a fairly stable percentage of the total population through 2050, when they are projected to compose 23 percent of the population.

Racial and ethnic diversity has grown in the United States, and the population is projected to become even more diverse in the decades to come. In 2023, less than half of all children are projected to be White, non-Hispanic (Figure 1). By 2050, 39 percent of U.S. children are projected to be Hispanic (up from 22 percent in 2009), and 38 percent are projected to be White, non-Hispanic (down from 55 percent in 2009).

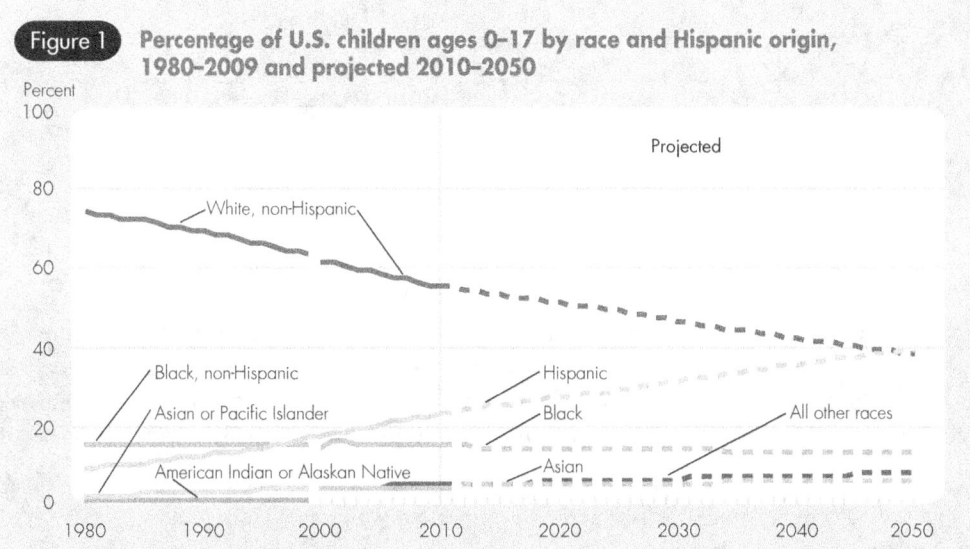

Figure 1 — Percentage of U.S. children ages 0–17 by race and Hispanic origin, 1980–2009 and projected 2010–2050

NOTE: Data from 2000 onward are not directly comparable with data from earlier years. Data on race and Hispanic origin are collected separately; Hispanics may be any race. In 1980 and 1990, following the 1977 Office of Management and Budget (OMB) standards for collecting and presenting data on race, the decennial census gave respondents the option to identify with one race from the following: White, Black, American Indian or Alaskan Native, or Asian or Pacific Islander. The Census Bureau also offered an "Other" category. Beginning in 2000, following the 1997 OMB standards for collecting and presenting data on race, the decennial census gave respondents the option to identify with one or more races from the following: White, Black, Asian, American Indian or Alaska Native, and Native Hawaiian or Other Pacific Islander. In addition, a "Some other race" category was included with OMB approval. Those who chose more than one race were classified as "Two or more races." Except for the "All other races" category, all race groups discussed from 2000 onward refer to people who indicated only one racial identity. (Those who were "Two or more races" were included in the "All other races" category, along with American Indians or Alaska Natives and Native Hawaiians or Other Pacific Islanders.)

SOURCE: U.S. Census Bureau, Population Estimates and Projections.

Family and Social Environment

This section presents information on children's families and the social environment in which they live, beginning with indicators on children's family composition and births to unmarried women. The indicators in this section also examine nativity, home language, child maltreatment, and adolescent births.

Family composition is dynamic and is associated with critical parental and economic resources. In 2009, 70 percent of children ages 0–17 lived with two parents,[1] 26 percent with one parent, and 4 percent with no parents (Figure 2). Among children living with two parents, 88 percent lived with two married parents (biological or adoptive). Among children living with one parent, 79 percent lived with their single mother (without a cohabiting partner). Among children living with neither parent, 52 percent lived with a grandparent. Six percent of all children ages 0–17 lived with a parent or parents who were cohabiting.

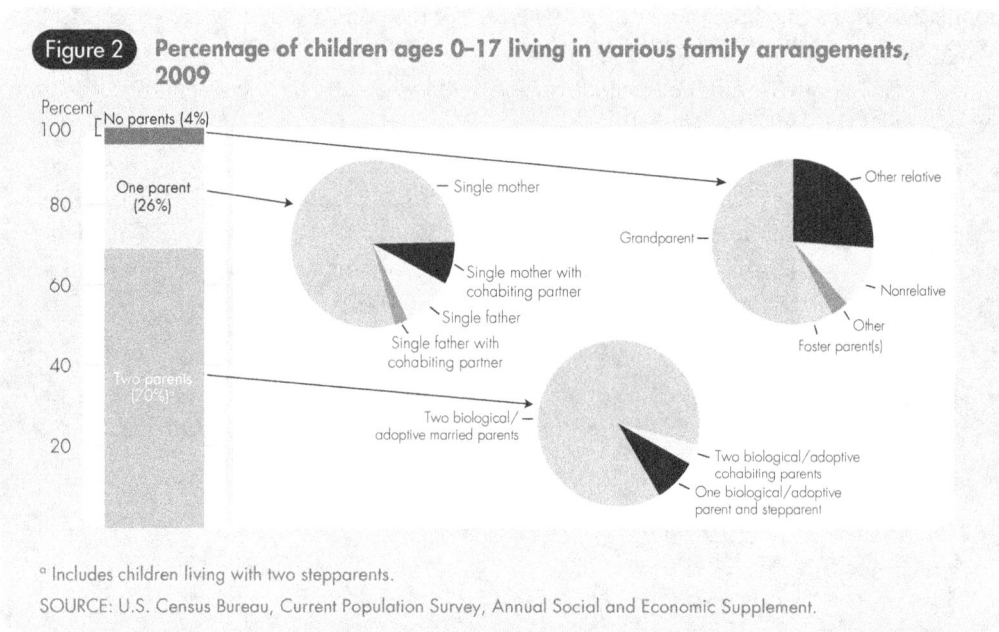

Figure 2 Percentage of children ages 0–17 living in various family arrangements, 2009

ª Includes children living with two stepparents.

SOURCE: U.S. Census Bureau, Current Population Survey, Annual Social and Economic Supplement.

A mother's marital status affects the family structure and economic security of her children.[2] The percentage of all births that were to unmarried women more than doubled between 1980 and 2008. In 2008, 41 percent of births were to unmarried women, up from 40 percent in 2007. Increases have occurred for women in all age groups, with the largest increases measured for women in their twenties.

While the percentage of all births that are to unmarried women has increased, the birth rate among unmarried women ages 15–44, a measure of the risk of a birth to an unmarried woman, decreased from 53 births per 1,000 unmarried women in 2007 to 52 births per 1,000 in 2008. During the years 2002–2007, the rate had increased more than one-fifth (44 to 53 births per 1,000), following relative stability between the mid-1990s and 2002.

In 2009, 19 percent of children ages 0–17 were native-born children with at least one foreign-born parent, and 3 percent were foreign-born children with at least one foreign-born parent. Overall, the percentage of all children living in the United States with at least one parent who was foreign-born rose from 15 percent in 1994 to 22 percent in 2009.

---

[1] Parents can be biological, step, or adoptive.

[2] National Center for Health Statistics, U.S. Department of Health and Human Services. (1995, September). *Report to Congress on out-of-wedlock childbearing* (DHHS Pub. No. [PHS] 95-1257). Hyattsville, MD: Author. Retrieved from http://www.cdc.gov/nchs/data/misc/wedlock.pdf.

Children who have difficulty speaking English may face greater challenges progressing in school and in the labor market. In 2008, 21 percent of children ages 5–17 spoke a language other than English at home, unchanged from 2007. The percentage of children who both spoke a language other than English at home and had difficulty speaking English (speak less than "very well") was 5.1 percent, down from 5.5 percent in 2000. In 2008, 16 percent of school-age Asian children and 17 percent of Hispanic children both spoke a language other than English at home and had difficulty speaking English.[3]

Child maltreatment comprises neglect (including medical neglect), as well as overt physical, sexual, and psychological abuse. In 2008, the rate of substantiated reports of child maltreatment[4] was 10 per 1,000 children ages 0–17. Children under age 1 experienced the highest rates of maltreatment: in 2008, there were 22 substantiated child maltreatment reports per 1,000 children under age 1.

In 2008, the adolescent birth rate[5] was 21.7 births per 1,000 young women ages 15–17 (135,733 births), down significantly from 22.2 births per 1,000 in 2007 (Figure 3). The rate had increased from 2005 to 2007, but from 1991 to 2005 the rate of adolescent childbearing had declined continuously (from 39 to 21 births per 1,000). Between 2007 and 2008, the adolescent birth rate declined for most race and ethnicity groups. The largest decline was reported for Hispanic adolescents, from 47.8 to 46.1 per 1,000, a record low. The rate for Black, non-Hispanic adolescents ages 15–17 decreased from 35.8 to 34.9 per 1,000 and the rate for White, non-Hispanic adolescents declined from 11.8 to 11.6 per 1,000. Changes for other groups were not statistically significant.

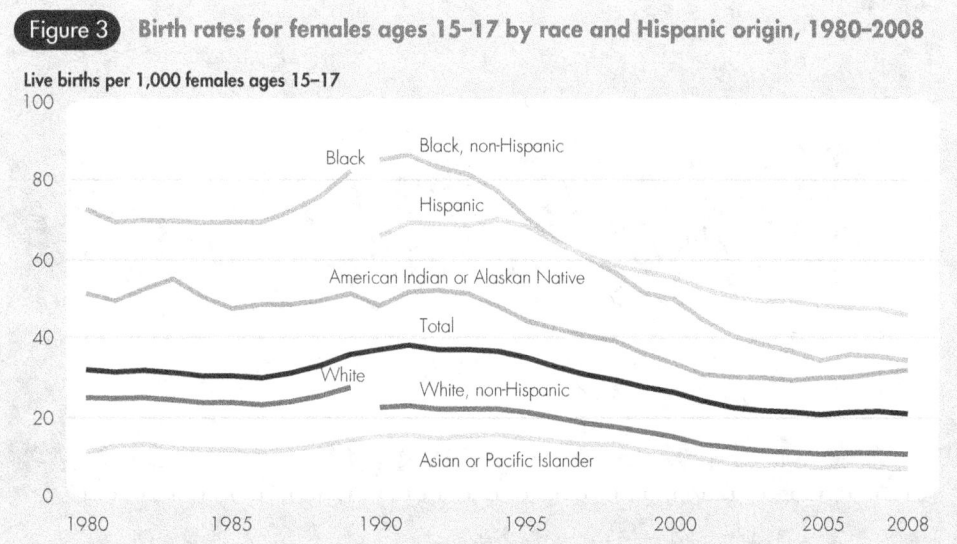

Figure 3   Birth rates for females ages 15-17 by race and Hispanic origin, 1980–2008

Live births per 1,000 females ages 15-17

NOTE: Data for 2007 and 2008 are preliminary. Race refers to mother's race. The 1977 Office of Management and Budget (OMB) Standards for Data on Race and Ethnicity were used to classify persons into one of the following four racial groups: White, Black, American Indian or Alaskan Native, or Asian or Pacific Islander. Although state reporting of birth certificate data is transitioning to comply with the 1997 OMB standard for race and ethnicity statistics, data from states reporting multiple races were bridged to the single-race categories of the 1977 OMB standards for comparability with other states and for trend analysis. Rates for 1980–1989 are not shown for Hispanics; White, non-Hispanics; or Black, non-Hispanics because information on Hispanic origin of the mother was not reported on birth certificates of most states and because population estimates by Hispanic ethnicity for the reporting states were not available. Data on race and Hispanic origin are collected and reported separately. Persons of Hispanic origin may be of any race.

SOURCE: National Center for Health Statistics, National Vital Statistics System.

---

[3]   In this survey, respondents were asked to choose one or more races. All race groups discussed in this paragraph refer to people who indicated only one racial identity. Hispanic children may be of any race.

[4]   The count of child victims is based on the number of investigations by Child Protective Services that found the child to be a victim of one or more types of maltreatment. The count of victims is, therefore, a report-based count and is a "duplicated count," since an individual child may have been maltreated more than once.

[5]   The birth rate for adolescents ages 15–17 includes married and unmarried teenagers.

Economic Circumstances

Measures of poverty,[6] secure parental employment, and food security offer insight into the material well-being of children and the economic factors that affect their health and development. These measures indicate that many children faced challenging economic circumstances in 2008.

In 2008, 19 percent of all children ages 0–17 (14.1 million) lived in poverty, an increase from 18 percent in 2007. Thus, nearly 1 in 5 children lived in poverty in 2008, the highest rate since 1998. Those in poverty included 1 in 10 White, non-Hispanic children (11 percent), more than 1 in 3 Black children (35 percent), and nearly 1 in 3 Hispanic children (31 percent).[7]

The percentage of related children[8] living in poverty also increased from 18 percent in 2007 to 19 percent in 2008, after fluctuating between 16 and 17 percent since 1999. For children in married-couple families, the percentage living in poverty increased from 9 percent in 2007 to 10 percent in 2008. Among Hispanic children in married-couple families, 22 percent lived in poverty, an increase from 19 percent in 2007.

In 2008, 8 percent of related children (5.9 million) lived in extreme poverty, defined as living in a family with income less than one-half of the poverty threshold (Figure 4). This percentage was the highest since 1998.

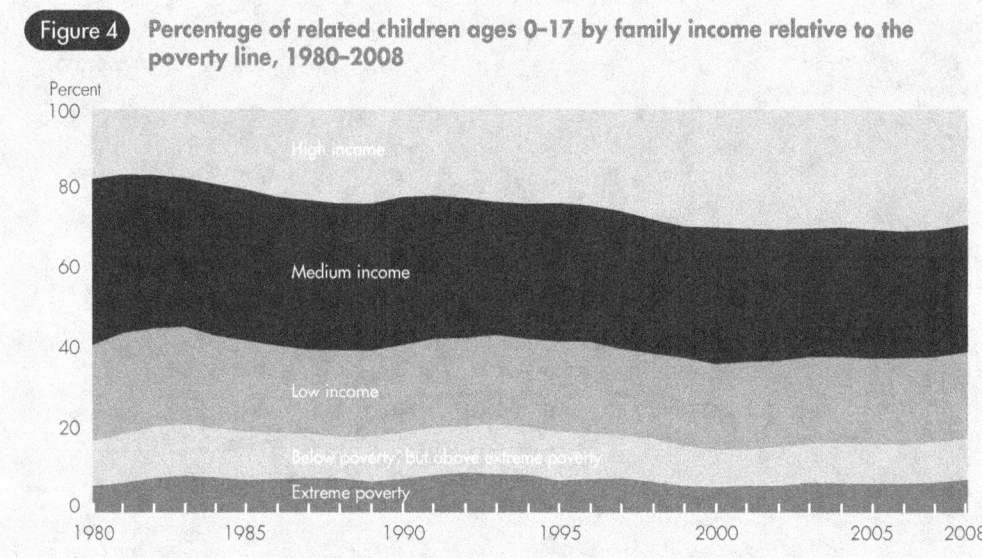

Figure 4 | **Percentage of related children ages 0–17 by family income relative to the poverty line, 1980–2008**

NOTE: Estimates refer to children ages 0–17 who are related to the householder. The income classes are derived from the ratio of the family's income to the family's poverty threshold. A child living in extreme poverty is defined as a child living in a family with income less than 50 percent of the poverty threshold. Below poverty, but above extreme poverty, is defined as 50–99 percent of the poverty threshold. Low income is defined as 100–199 percent of the poverty threshold. Medium income is defined as 200–399 percent of the poverty threshold. High income is defined as being at or above 400 percent of the poverty threshold. For example, in 2008, a family of four with two children would be in extreme poverty if their income was less than $10,917 (50 percent of $21,834). The same family would be classified as low income if their income was at least $21,834 and less than $43,668.

SOURCE: U.S. Census Bureau, Current Population Survey, Annual Social and Economic Supplements.

---

[6] Following Office of Management and Budget Statistical Policy Directive 14, poverty status is determined by comparing a family's (or an unrelated individual's) income to one of 48 dollar amounts called thresholds. The thresholds vary by the size of the family and the members' ages. In 2008, the poverty threshold for a family with two adults and two children was $21,834. For further details, see http://www.census.gov/hhes/www/poverty/poverty.html.

[7] In this survey, respondents were asked to choose one or more races. All race groups discussed in this paragraph refer to people who indicated only one racial identity. Hispanic children may be of any race.

[8] Official poverty estimates for children are compiled in two ways—estimates for all children for whom poverty status can be determined and estimates for related children. Related children are related to the householder (or a subfamily reference person) by birth, marriage, or adoption and are not themselves householders, spouses, or reference persons. In 2008, all children included an additional 1.1 million children ages 15–17 who were not related to the householder.

America's Children in Brief: Key National Indicators of Well-Being, 2010

Secure parental employment reduces the incidence of poverty and its related risks for children. The percentage of children with at least one parent working year round, full time was 75 percent in 2008, a decrease from 77 percent in 2007. The 2008 estimate for secure parental employment was the lowest since 1996. In 2008, 77 percent of older children (ages 6–17) had at least one parent who worked year round, full time, compared with only 71 percent of younger children (ages 0–5).

A family's ability to provide for its children's nutritional needs is linked to the family's food security—that is, to its access at all times to enough food for active, healthy lives for all family members. About 22 percent of children lived in households that were food insecure at times in 2008, an increase from 17 percent in 2007 and the highest percentage recorded since monitoring began in 1995 (Figure 5).[9] About 1.5 percent of children (1.1 million) in 2008 lived in households with very low food security among children,[10] up from 0.9 percent in 2007.

In 2008, among children living in households with incomes below the poverty threshold, 52 percent were in food-insecure households. Among children living in households with incomes at 100–199 percent of the poverty threshold (low income), 34 percent were in food-insecure households; and among children in households with incomes at or above 200 percent of the poverty threshold (medium and high income), about 9 percent were in food-insecure households.

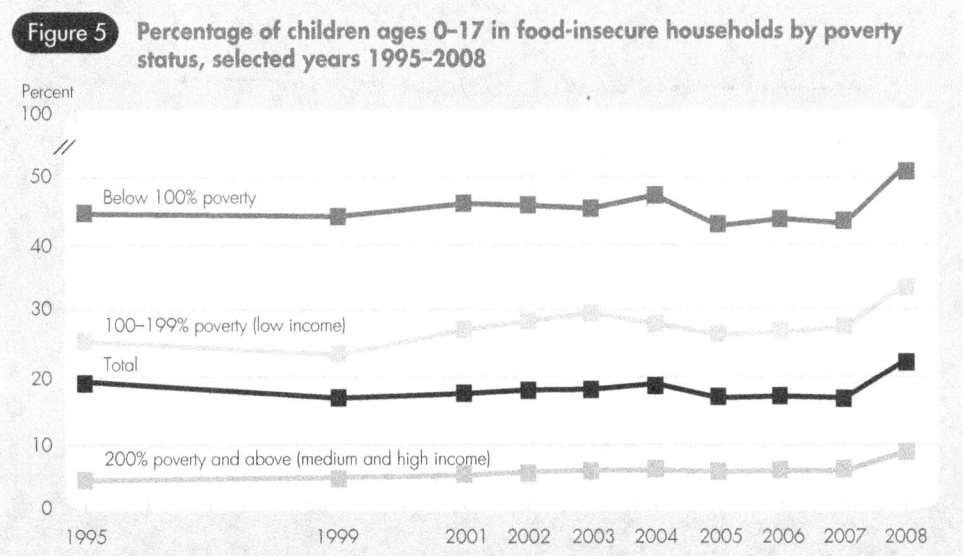

Figure 5 Percentage of children ages 0–17 in food-insecure households by poverty status, selected years 1995–2008

NOTE: Food-insecure households are those in which either adults or children or both were "food insecure," meaning that, at times, they were unable to acquire adequate food for active, healthy living for all household members because they had insufficient money and other resources for food. Statistics for 1996–1998 and 2000 are omitted because they are not directly comparable with those for other years.

SOURCE: U.S. Census Bureau, Current Population Survey Food Security Supplement; tabulated by U.S. Department of Agriculture, Economic Research Service and Food and Nutrition Service.

---

[9] The food security status of households is assessed based on self-reports of difficulty in obtaining enough food, reduced food intake, reduced diet quality, and anxiety about an adequate food supply. In some households classified as food insecure, only adults' diets and food intakes were affected, but in a majority of such households, children's eating patterns were also disrupted to some extent and the quality and variety of their diets were adversely affected. See Nord, M. (2009). *Food insecurity in households with children: Prevalence, severity, and household characteristics* (Economic Information Bulletin No. 56). Washington, DC: U.S. Department of Agriculture, Economic Research Service. Retrieved from http://www.ers.usda.gov/Publications/EIB56/.

[10] In households classified as having very low food security among children, a parent or guardian reported that at some time during the year one or more children were hungry, skipped a meal, or did not eat for a whole day because the household could not afford enough food.

Health Care

Health care includes the prevention, treatment, and management of illness and the promotion of mental and physical well-being through services offered by health professionals. Effective health care is an important aspect of promoting good health. The following indicators include measures of access to health care (health insurance and usual source of care) and indicators of two types of health care utilization (oral health and childhood immunization).

Children with health insurance, whether public or private, are more likely than children without insurance to have a regular and accessible source of health care. In 2008, 90 percent of children had health insurance coverage at least some time during the year, up from 89 percent in 2007 (Figure 6). The number of children without coverage at any time during the year was 7.3 million (10 percent of all children).[11] The percentage of children with public health insurance increased from 31 percent in 2007 to 33 percent in 2008.

In 2008, Hispanic children were less likely to have health insurance, compared with White, non-Hispanic or Black children.[12] Specifically, 83 percent of Hispanic children were covered by health insurance at some time during the year, compared with 93 percent of White, non-Hispanic children and 89 percent of Black children.

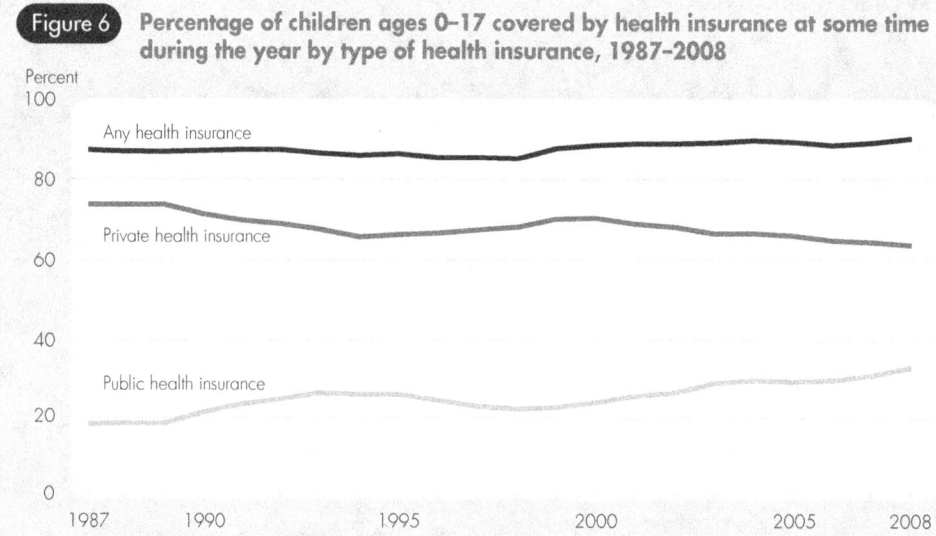

Figure 6 — Percentage of children ages 0–17 covered by health insurance at some time during the year by type of health insurance, 1987–2008

NOTE: Public health insurance for children consists primarily of Medicaid, but also includes Medicare, State Children's Health Insurance Programs (SCHIP), and CHAMPUS/Tricare, the health benefit program for members of the armed forces and their dependents. Estimates beginning in 1999 include follow-up questions to verify health insurance status. Children are considered to be covered by health insurance if they had public or private coverage any time during the year. The data from 1996 to 2004 have been revised since initially published. For more information, see http://www.census.gov/hhes/www/hlthins/usernote/schedule.html.

SOURCE: U.S. Census Bureau, unpublished tables from the Current Population Survey, Annual Social and Economic Supplements.

Having a usual source of care—a particular person or place a child goes for sick and preventive care—facilitates the timely and appropriate use of pediatric services.[13] In 2008, 6 percent of children had no usual source of health care; this was similar to the percentage in 2007. Children who were uninsured were nearly 10 times more likely than those with private insurance to not have a usual source of care in 2008 (30 percent, compared with about 3 percent).

---

[11] DeNavas Walt, C., Proctor, B.D., and Smith, J.C. (2009, September). *Income, poverty, and health insurance coverage in the United States: 2008* (Current Population Reports, P60-236[RV]). Washington, DC: U.S. Census Bureau. Retrieved from http://www.census.gov/prod/2009pubs/p60-236.pdf.

[12] In this survey, respondents were asked to choose one or more races. All race groups discussed in this paragraph refer to people who indicated only one racial identity. Hispanic children may be of any race.

[13] Foltin, G.L. (1995). Critical issues in urban emergency medical services for children. *Pediatrics, 96*(1), 174–179.

Dental caries (cavities) is the single most common chronic disease of childhood.[14] The percentage of younger children (ages 5–11) with untreated dental caries declined to 20 percent in 2005–2008 from 27 percent in 1999–2004 (Figure 7). For older children (ages 12–17) the percentage declined to 12 percent in 2005–2008 from 19 percent in 1999–2004. In 2005–2008, the percentage of both younger and older children with untreated dental caries living below the poverty level was twice that of children in families with incomes at or above 200 percent of the poverty level. From 1999–2004 to 2005–2008 the percentage of children with untreated dental caries significantly declined for children living below the poverty level and for children in families with incomes at 100–199 percent of the poverty level.

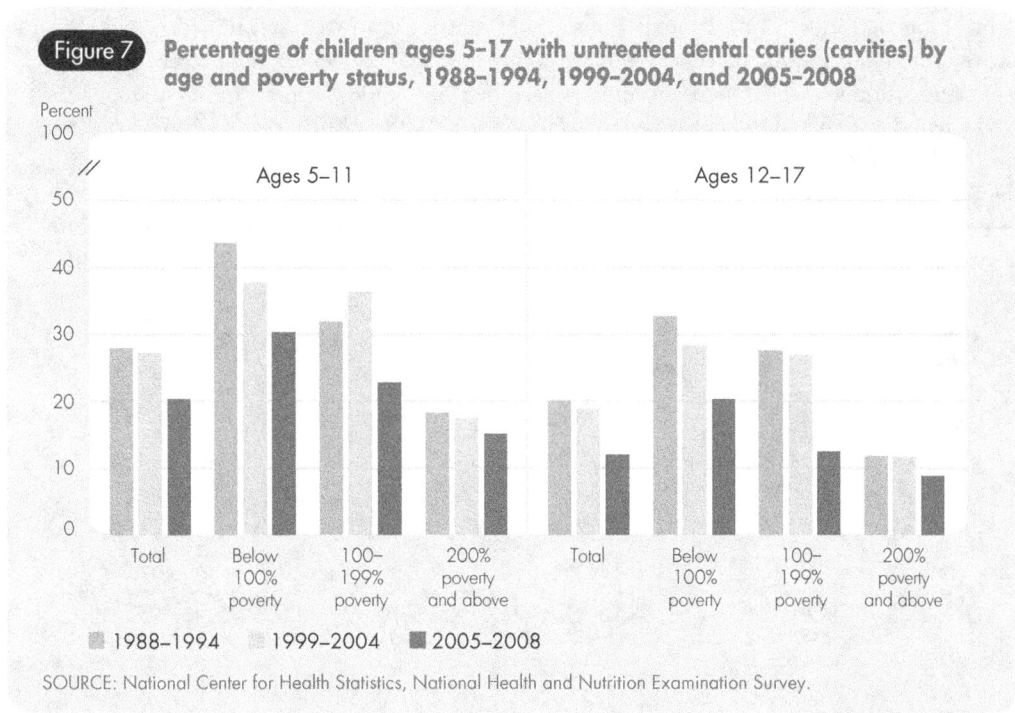

Figure 7   **Percentage of children ages 5–17 with untreated dental caries (cavities) by age and poverty status, 1988–1994, 1999–2004, and 2005–2008**

SOURCE: National Center for Health Statistics, National Health and Nutrition Examination Survey.

Immunization coverage rates measure another aspect of health promotion—the extent to which children are being protected from vaccine-preventable diseases. In 2008, 76 percent of children ages 19–35 months received the recommended combined six-vaccine series (often referred to as the 4:3:1:3:3:1 combined series).[15] Children in families living below the poverty level had a lower rate of coverage (72 percent) with the combined six-vaccine series than children in families living at or above the poverty level (78 percent).

The percentage of children ages 19–35 months who received the recommended four doses (or more) of pneumococcal conjugate vaccine (PCV) increased from 75 percent in 2007 to 80 percent in 2008. The Hepatitis A vaccine was universally recommended in 2006, and 40 percent of children ages 19–35 months received the recommended two doses (or more) of the vaccine in 2008.

---

14   Dye, B.A., Arevalo, O., and Vargas, C.M. (2010). Trends in paediatric caries by poverty status in the United States, 1988–1994 and 1999–2004. *International Journal of Paediatric Dentistry, 20*(2): 132–143.

15   The 4:3:1:3:3:1 series consists of 4 doses (or more) of diphtheria, tetanus toxoids, and pertussis (DTP) vaccines, diphtheria and tetanus toxoids (DT), or diphtheria, tetanus toxoids, and any acellular pertussis (DTaP) vaccines; 3 doses (or more) of poliovirus vaccines; 1 dose (or more) of any measles-containing vaccine; 3 doses (or more) of *Haemophilus influenzae* type b (Hib) vaccines; 3 doses (or more) of hepatitis B vaccines; and 1 dose (or more) of varicella vaccine. The collection of coverage rate estimates for this series began in 2002. The recommended immunization schedule for children is available at http://www.cdc.gov/vaccines/recs/schedules/child-schedule.htm#printable.

Physical Environment and Safety

The physical environment in which children develop should be healthy and safe from hazardous conditions. Indicators of environmental safety include exposure to indoor air pollutants, drinking water contaminants, and lead. The physical environment is also measured by housing problems and violent crime victimization.

Children's exposure to indoor air pollutants can have a substantial impact on their health.[16] Exposure to secondhand smoke increases the probability of lower respiratory tract infections, asthma, other respiratory conditions, and sudden infant death syndrome (SIDS).[17] Cotinine, a breakdown product of nicotine, is a marker for recent exposure to secondhand smoke. As the number of public places allowing smoking has declined, so has the percentage of children with detectable blood cotinine levels.[18] In 2007–2008, 53 percent of children ages 4–11 had detectable blood cotinine levels (at or above 0.05 ng/mL), down from 64 percent in 1999–2000 and 88 percent in 1988–1994 (Figure 8). The percentage of children with blood cotinine levels above 1.0 ng/mL, which indicates high levels of secondhand smoke exposure at home or other places, declined from 26 percent in 1988–1994 to 18 percent in 1999–2000.[19] The percentage did not change significantly from 1999–2000 to 2007–2008.

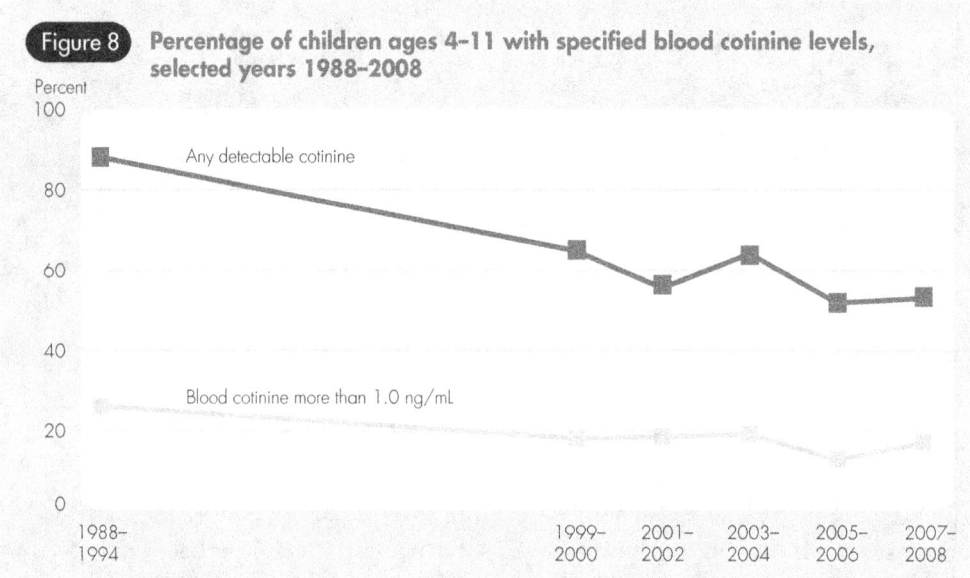

Figure 8 Percentage of children ages 4–11 with specified blood cotinine levels, selected years 1988–2008

NOTE: "Any detectable cotinine" indicates blood cotinine levels at or above 0.05 nanograms per milliliter (ng/mL), the detectable level of cotinine in the blood in 1988–1994. Cotinine levels are reported for nonsmoking children only. The average (geometric mean) blood cotinine level in children living in homes where someone smoked was 1.0 ng/mL in 1988–1994 and in 2003–2006.[19]

SOURCE: National Center for Health Statistics, National Health and Nutrition Examination Survey.

Children are particularly sensitive to some contaminants in drinking water, which may cause acute diseases such as gastrointestinal illness, developmental effects such as learning disorders, and serious long-term illnesses such as cancer.[20] The percentage of children served

16   Esmen, N.A. (1985). The status of indoor air pollution. *Environmental Health Perspectives, 62*, 259–265.

17   U.S. Department of Health and Human Services. (2006). *The health consequences of involuntary exposure to tobacco smoke: A report of the Surgeon General.* Atlanta, GA: Centers for Disease Control and Prevention. Retrieved from http://www.surgeongeneral.gov/library/secondhandsmoke/.

18   Eriksen, M.P., and Cerak, R.L. (2008). The diffusion and impact of clean indoor air laws. *Annual Review of Public Health, 29*, 171–185.

19   Mannino, D.M., Caraballo, R., Benowitz, N., and Repace, J. (2001). Predictors of cotinine levels in U.S. children: Data from the Third National Health and Nutrition Examination Survey. *CHEST, 120*, 718–724. Marano, C., Schober, S.E., Brody, D.J., and Zhang, C. (2009). Secondhand tobacco smoke exposure among children and adolescents: United States, 2003–2006. *Pediatrics, 124*(5): 1299–1305.

20   U.S. Environmental Protection Agency. (2009). *Drinking water contaminants.* EPA Office of Water. Retrieved from http://www.epa.gov/safewater/hfacts.html. U.S. Environmental Protection Agency. (2009). *America's children and the environment (ACE): Environmental contaminants: Violations of drinking water standards.* Retrieved from http://www.epa.gov/envirohealth/children/contaminants/e6-background.html.

by community drinking water systems that did not meet all applicable health-based standards has fluctuated between 5 and 12 percent since 1995, and was 6 percent in 2008.

Blood lead levels in children ages 1–5 continue to drop. For 2005–2008, the sample of children was too small to provide a statistically reliable estimate of the percentage of children with a blood lead level greater than 10 micrograms per deciliter (µg/dL) (Figure 9). Three percent of children had levels at or above 5 µg/dL, and 16 percent had levels at or above 2.5 µg/dL. For Black, non-Hispanic children, who have the highest blood lead levels among all racial and ethnic groups, lead levels at or above 5 µg/dL declined from 19 percent of children in 1999–2002[21] to 7 percent in 2005–2008, and levels at or above 2.5 µg/dL fell from 54 percent to 32 percent.[22] There is no "safe" blood lead level: on average, children's IQ scores decrease 6 points as blood lead levels increase from 0 to 10 µg/dL.[23]

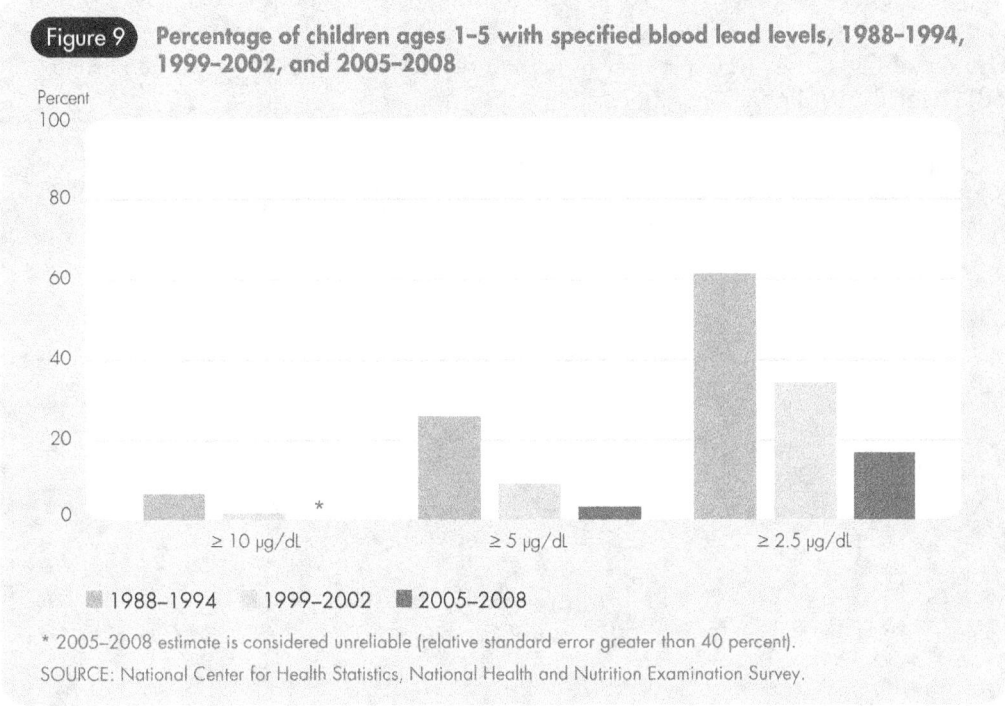

Figure 9 Percentage of children ages 1–5 with specified blood lead levels, 1988–1994, 1999–2002, and 2005–2008

Percent

■ 1988–1994   ■ 1999–2002   ■ 2005–2008

* 2005–2008 estimate is considered unreliable (relative standard error greater than 40 percent).

SOURCE: National Center for Health Statistics, National Health and Nutrition Examination Survey.

Inadequate, unhealthy, crowded, or too-costly housing can pose serious problems for children's physical, psychological, and material well-being.[24] In 2007, 43 percent of U.S. households with children had physically inadequate housing, crowded housing, and/or a housing cost burden of more than 30 percent of household income.[25] Cost burdens have driven significant increases in the overall incidence of housing problems over the long term and especially since 2003, when 37 percent of households with children had one or more of these problems.

Another measure of children's safety is their violent crime victimization rate. In 2008, the rate at which youth were victims of serious violent crimes was 12 crimes per 1,000 juveniles ages 12–17. This rate is similar to the victimization rate in 2007, but significantly lower than in 1993, when the serious violent crime victimization rate was 44 per 1,000 juveniles (the highest since 1980).

[21] Federal Interagency Forum on Child and Family Statistics. *America's children: Key national indicators of well-being, 2005.* Washington, DC: U.S. Government Printing Office. Retrieved from http://childstats.gov.

[22] In this survey, respondents were asked to choose one or more races. All race groups discussed in this paragraph refer to people who indicated only one racial identity. Hispanic children may be of any race.

[23] Lanphear, B.P., Hornung, R., Khoury, J., Yolton, K., Baghurst, P., Bellinger, D.C., . . . Roberts, R. (2005). Low-level environmental lead exposure and children's intellectual function: An international pooled analysis. *Environmental Health Perspectives, 113*(7): 894–899.

[24] Breysse, P., Farr, N., Galke, W., Lanphear, B., Morley, R., Bergofsky, L. (2004). The relationship between housing and health: Children at risk. *Environmental Health Perspectives, 112*(15), 1583–1588. Krieger, J., and Higgins, D.L. (2002). Housing and health: Time again for public health action. *American Journal of Public Health 92*(5), 758–68.

[25] Paying 30 percent or more of income for housing may leave insufficient resources for other basic needs. See Panel on Poverty and Family Assistance, National Research Council. (1995). *Measuring poverty: A new approach.* Washington, DC: National Academy Press. Retrieved from http://www.census.gov/hhes/www/povmeas/toc.html.

Behavior

Adolescent participation in high-risk or illegal behaviors can have severe, long-term consequences for the individuals, their families, and for society. Substance use behaviors include smoking cigarettes, drinking alcohol, and using illicit drugs. Other risky behaviors include early sexual activity and participation in violent crime.

Smoking has serious long-term consequences, including the risk of smoking-related diseases and premature death.[26] In addition, there are increased health care costs associated with treating smoking-related disease. The percentage of adolescents who smoke regularly has reached its lowest level since monitoring began. In 2009, less than 3 percent of 8th-graders reported smoking cigarettes daily (Figure 10). This percentage is a decline from the peak in 1996, when over 10 percent of 8th-graders reported smoking cigarettes daily. In 2009, 6 percent of 10th-graders and 11 percent of 12th-graders reported smoking cigarettes daily—down from peaks of 18 percent of 10th-graders in 1996 and 25 percent of 12th-graders in 1997.

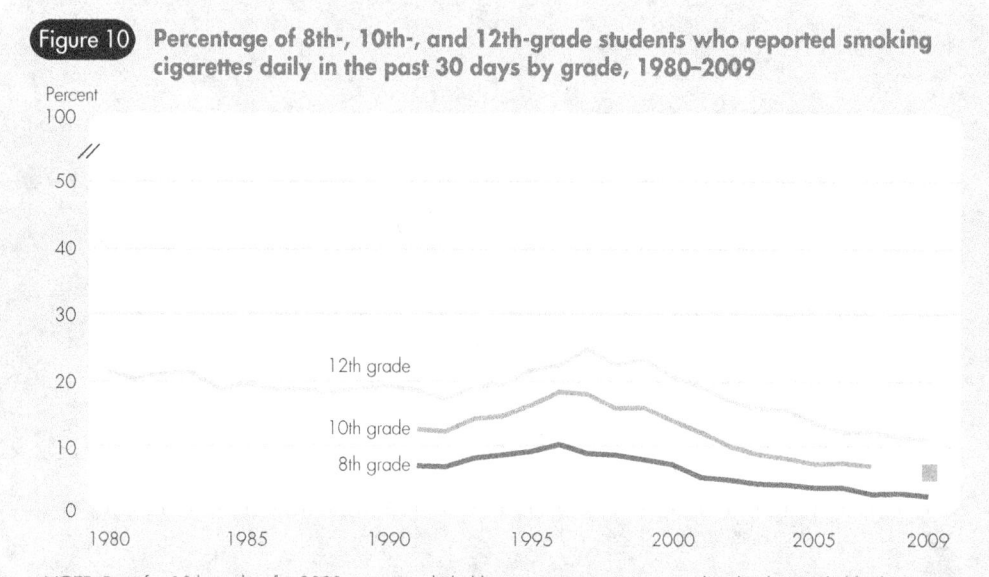

Figure 10 Percentage of 8th-, 10th-, and 12th-grade students who reported smoking cigarettes daily in the past 30 days by grade, 1980–2009

NOTE: Data for 10th-graders for 2008 are not included because estimates are considered to be unreliable due to sampling error. See http://www.monitoringthefuture.org/data/09data.html#2009data-drugs.

SOURCE: National Institute on Drug Abuse, Monitoring the Future Survey.

Alcohol use by adolescents can also have severe consequences; it is associated with problems in school, fighting, crime, and motor vehicle accidents, injuries, and deaths.[27] Early onset of heavy drinking, defined here as five or more alcoholic beverages in a row during a single occasion in the previous 2 weeks, may be especially problematic, potentially increasing the likelihood of these negative outcomes. Between 1999 and 2009, heavy drinking declined from 13 percent to 8 percent among 8th-graders, from 24 percent to 18 percent among 10th-graders, and from 31 percent to 25 percent among 12th-graders. In 2009, 8 percent of White, non-Hispanic, 5 percent of Black, non-Hispanic, and 12 percent of Hispanic 8th-grade students reported heavy drinking.[28] Among 10th-graders, 18 percent of White, non-Hispanic students, 10 percent of Black, non-Hispanic students, and 21 percent of Hispanic students reported heavy drinking. The percentages of White, non-Hispanic,

---

[26] U.S. Department of Health and Human Services. (2004). *The health consequences of smoking: A report of the Surgeon General.* Washington, DC: Government Printing Office. Retrieved from http://www.cdc.gov/tobacco/data_statistics/sgr/2004/index.htm/.

[27] National Institute on Alcohol Abuse and Alcoholism. (2004/2005). Alcohol and development in youth—A multidisciplinary overview. *Alcohol Research & Health, 28*(3): 107–176. Retrieved from http://pubs.niaaa.nih.gov/publications/arh283/toc28-3.htm.

[28] In this survey, respondents were asked to choose one or more races. All race groups discussed in this paragraph refer to people who indicated only one racial identity. Hispanic children may be of any race.

Black, non-Hispanic, and Hispanic 12th-grade students reporting heavy drinking in 2009 were 29 percent, 12 percent, and 23 percent, respectively.

Illicit drug use is a risk-taking behavior that has potentially serious negative consequences. Recent illicit drug use among youth remained unchanged from 2008 to 2009. In 2009, 8 percent of 8th-graders, 18 percent of 10th-graders, and 23 percent of 12th-graders reported illicit drug use in the past 30 days. These statistics represent declines from peaks of 15 percent for 8th-graders and 23 percent for 10th-graders in 1996 and 26 percent for 12th-graders in 1997.

Early sexual activity is associated with emotional[29] and physical health risks. Youth who engage in sexual activity are at risk of contracting sexually transmitted infections (STIs) and becoming pregnant. In 2007, 48 percent of high school students reported ever having had sexual intercourse. In the same year, among those reporting having had sexual intercourse during the past 3 months, 16 percent reported the use of birth control pills to prevent pregnancy before the last sexual intercourse and 62 percent reported use of a condom during the last sexual intercourse.

One measure of youth violence in society is the rate of serious crimes committed by youth perpetrators. In 2008, the serious violent crime offending rate was 14 crimes per 1,000 juveniles ages 12–17, totaling 343,000 such crimes involving juveniles (Figure 11). The percentage of all serious violent crimes which involved youth offenders has ranged from 16 percent in 2002 to 26 percent in 1993, the peak year for youth violence. In 2008, 22 percent of all such victimizations reportedly involved a juvenile offender.

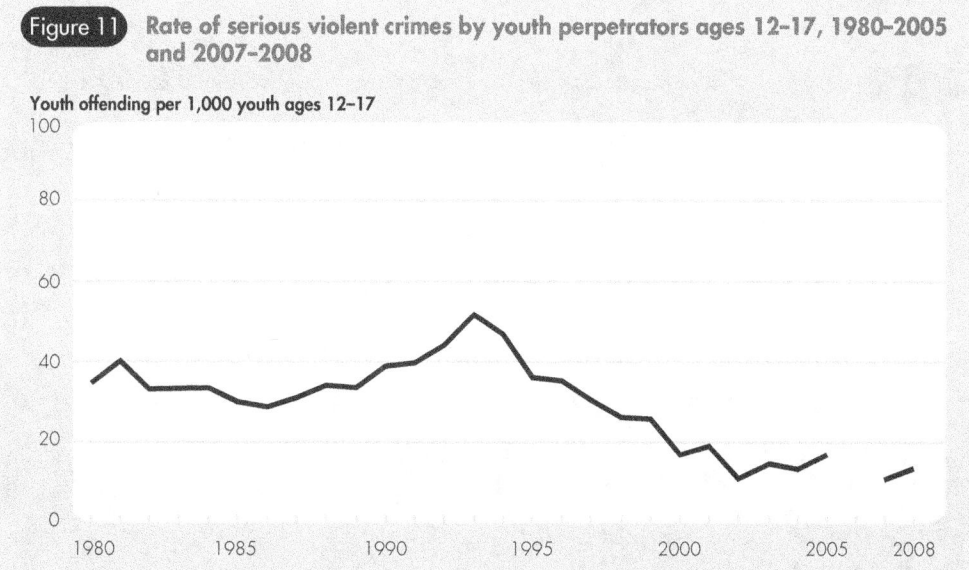

Figure 11 Rate of serious violent crimes by youth perpetrators ages 12-17, 1980-2005 and 2007-2008

Youth offending per 1,000 youth ages 12–17

NOTE: The offending rate is the ratio of the number of crimes (aggravated assault, rape, and robbery, i.e., stealing by force or threat of violence) reported to the National Crime Victimization Survey that involved at least one offender perceived by the victim to be 12–17 years of age, plus the number of homicides reported to the police that involved at least one juvenile offender, to the number of juveniles in the population. Homicide data were not available for 2008 at the time of publication. The number of homicides for 2007 is included in the overall total for 2008. In 2007, homicides represented less than 1 percent of serious violent crime, and the total number of homicides by juveniles has been relatively stable over the last decade. Because of changes made in the victimization survey, data prior to 1992 are adjusted to make them comparable with data collected under the redesigned methodology. Data from 2006 are not included because, due to changes in methodology, 2006 crime perpetration rates are not comparable to other years and cannot be used for yearly trend comparisons. See *Criminal Victimization, 2006*, http://bjs.ojp.usdoj.gov/index.cfm?ty=pbdetail&iid=765.

SOURCE: Bureau of Justice Statistics, National Crime Victimization Survey and Federal Bureau of Investigation, Uniform Crime Reporting Program, Supplementary Homicide Reports.

[29]   Meier, A.M. (2007). Adolescent first sex and subsequent mental health. *American Journal of Sociology 112*(6): 1811–1847.

Education

Education shapes the personal growth and life chances of our children, as well as the economic and social progress of our Nation. Early educational experiences of young children, such as being read to daily, encourage the development of essential skills and prepare children for success in school. Later aspects of academic performance, such as mastering academic subjects, completing high school, and enrolling in college, provide opportunities for further education and future employment. Youth who are neither enrolled in school nor working is a measure of the proportion of young people at risk of limiting their future prospects.

In 2007, 55 percent of children ages 3–5 who were not yet in kindergarten were read to daily by a family member. The percentage of children in families with incomes at or above 200 percent of the poverty level who were read to daily was 64 percent in 2007. This was higher than the percentages of children in families with incomes below the poverty level (40 percent) or those in families with incomes at 100–199 percent of the poverty level (50 percent).

The National Assessment of Educational Progress (NAEP) measures national trends in student performance in mathematics, reading, and other academic subjects. The average 4th-grade NAEP mathematics score in 2009 was higher than the score in 1990, but unchanged from the score in 2007 (Figure 12). The average 8th-grade mathematics score in 2009 was higher than the score in all previous assessment years and 2 points higher than the score in 2007. The average NAEP reading score at grade 4 increased by 4 points, from 217 to 221 (on a scale of 0–500) between 1992 and 2009, but was unchanged from the average score in 2007. At grade 8, the 2009 average reading score (264) was 4 points higher than the score in 1992 and 1 point higher than the average score in 2007.

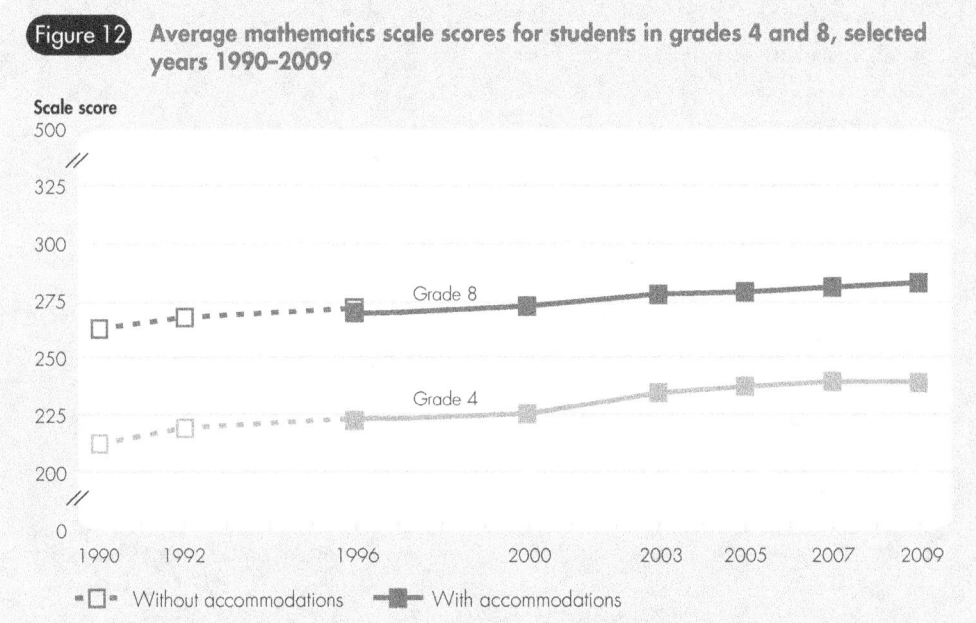

Figure 12 Average mathematics scale scores for students in grades 4 and 8, selected years 1990–2009

Scale score

- - □ - - Without accommodations   ▪-■-▪ With accommodations

NOTE: Data are available for 1990, 1992, 1996, 2000, 2003, 2005, 2007, and 2009. In early years of the assessment, testing accommodations (e.g., extended time, small group testing) for children with disabilities and limited-English-proficient students were not permitted. In 1996, scores are shown for both the assessments with and without accommodations to show comparability across the assessments.

SOURCE: U.S. Department of Education, National Center for Education Statistics, National Assessment of Educational Progress.

Detachment from school and employment, activities that usually occupy teenagers, puts youth at increased risk of having lower earnings and a less stable employment history than their peers who stayed in school, secured jobs, or both.[30] In an average week during the 2009 school year, 9 percent of youth ages 16–19 were neither enrolled in school nor working (Figure 13). Black, non-Hispanic (12 percent) and Hispanic (13 percent) youth were more likely to be neither enrolled nor working than were White, non-Hispanic youth (7 percent). In 2009, youth ages 18–19 were more than three times as likely to be detached from school and work activities as youth ages 16–17 (15 percent vs. 4 percent).

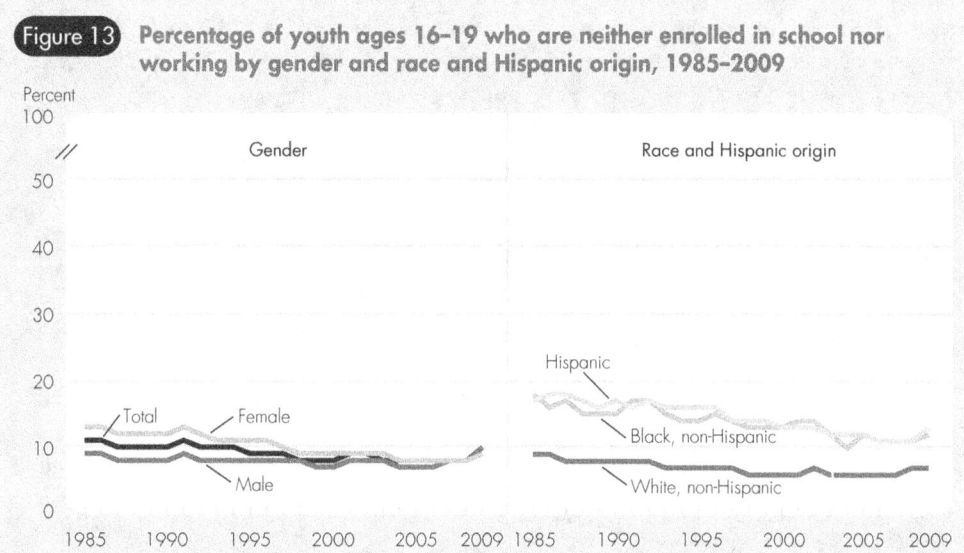

Figure 13 Percentage of youth ages 16–19 who are neither enrolled in school nor working by gender and race and Hispanic origin, 1985–2009

NOTE: The information relates to the labor force and enrollment status of persons 16–19 years old in the civilian noninstitutionalized population during an "average" week of the school year. School refers to both high school and college. For data before 2003, the 1977 Office of Management and Budget (OMB) Standards for Data on Race and Ethnicity were used to classify persons into one of the following four racial groups: White, Black, American Indian or Alaskan Native, or Asian or Pacific Islander. The revised 1997 OMB standards were used for data for 2003 and later years. Persons could select one or more of five racial groups: White, Black or African American, American Indian or Alaska Native, Asian, or Native Hawaiian or Other Pacific Islander. Beginning in 2003, those in each racial category represent those reporting only one race. Data from 2003 onward are not directly comparable with data from earlier years. Data on race and Hispanic origin are collected separately. Persons of Hispanic origin may be of any race.

SOURCE: U.S. Bureau of Labor Statistics, Current Population Survey.

In 2008, 90 percent of young adults ages 18–24 had completed high school. This represents an increase from 1980, when 84 percent had completed high school.[31] During this period, the high school completion rate increased from 88 to 94 percent for White, non-Hispanics and from 75 to 87 percent for Black, non-Hispanics.[32] While the rate for Hispanic young adults has been consistently lower than for other racial and ethnic groups, it increased from 57 percent in 1980 to 76 percent in 2008.

In 2008, 69 percent of high school completers enrolled in a 2-year or 4-year college immediately after high school graduation, an increase from 49 percent in 1980. Between 1980 and 2008, the immediate enrollment rate of high school completers increased from 50 to 72 percent for White, non-Hispanics and from 43 to 56 percent for Black, non-Hispanics. Among Hispanics,[33] the immediate enrollment rate fluctuated between 1980 and 1999. Since 1999, the moving average for Hispanics has increased steadily, from 48 percent in 1999 to 62 percent in 2007.

---

[30] Brown, B. (1996). *Who are America's disconnected youth?* Report prepared for the American Enterprise Institute. Washington, DC: Child Trends, Inc.

[31] Refers to those who completed 12 years of school for survey years 1980–1991 and to those who earned a high school diploma or equivalent (e.g., a General Educational Development [GED] certificate) for all years since 1992.

[32] In this survey, respondents were asked to choose one or more races. All race groups discussed in this paragraph refer to people who indicated only one racial identity. Hispanic young adults may be of any race.

[33] Due to small sample sizes, a 3-year moving average is used to measure the trend for Hispanics.

Health

Children's health is influenced by their biology, social and physical environment, and behavior, as well as the availability of services. This section presents information about indicators related to birth outcomes and key physical and mental health conditions that may result from a combination of these influences.

Infants born preterm or with low birthweight[34] are at high risk of early death and long-term health and developmental problems.[35] Following many years of increases, the U.S. preterm birth rate declined for the second straight year, from 12.8 percent in 2006 to 12.7 percent in 2007 to 12.3 percent in 2008. Decreases in preterm rates between 2007 and 2008 were seen for each of the three largest race and ethnicity groups: White, non-Hispanic, Black, non-Hispanic, and Hispanic women.[36] The 2008 low birthweight rate was 8.2 percent, unchanged from 2007. The low birthweight rate had fallen slightly between 2006 and 2007 (from 8.3 percent).

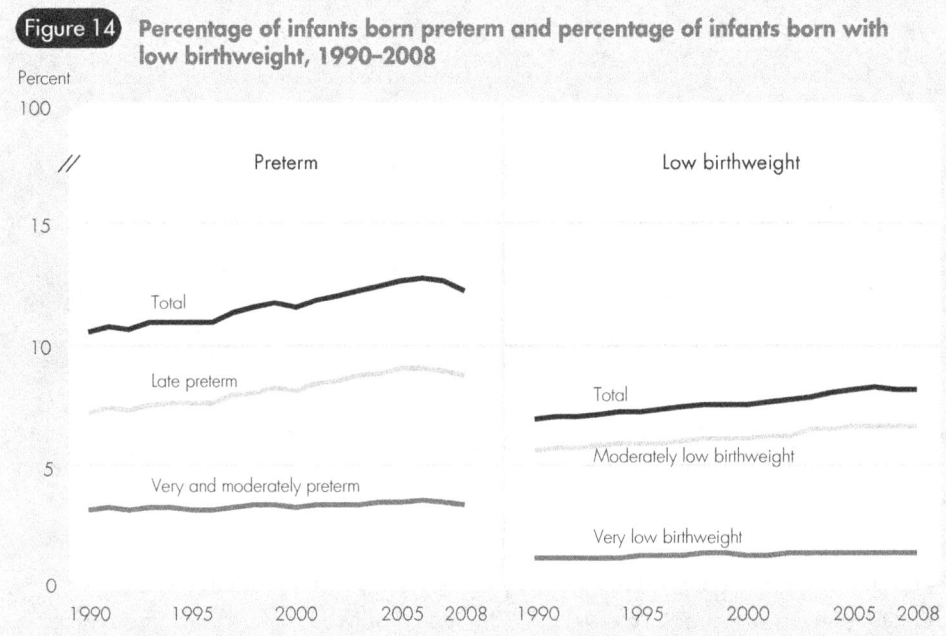

Figure 14 Percentage of infants born preterm and percentage of infants born with low birthweight, 1990–2008

NOTE: Data for 2007 and 2008 are preliminary. Late preterm infants are born at 34–36 weeks of gestation; very and moderately preterm infants are born at less than 34 weeks gestation. Moderately low birthweight infants weigh 1,500–2,499 grams at birth; very low birthweight infants weigh less than 1,500 grams at birth.

SOURCE: National Center for Health Statistics, National Vital Statistics System.

Asthma is one of the most common chronic diseases among children. In 2008, 9 percent of children had current asthma, which includes children with active asthma symptoms and children with well-controlled asthma. The percentage of children with current asthma increased slightly from 2001 to 2008.

The percentage of children who are obese is a public health challenge. In 1976–1980, only 6 percent of children ages 6–17 were obese.[37] This percentage rose to 11 percent in 1988–1994

---

[34]   Preterm births are births less than 37 weeks gestation. Low birthweight infants weigh less than 2,500 grams, or 5 lbs. 8 oz. at birth.

[35]   Institute of Medicine, Committee on Understanding Premature Birth and Assuring Healthy Outcomes and Board on Health Sciences Policy. (2005). *Preterm birth: Causes, consequences, and prevention.* R.E. Behrman and A.S. Butler. (Eds). Washington, DC: The National Academies Press. Retrieved from http://www.iom.edu/~/media/Files/Report%20Files/2006/Preterm-Birth-Causes-Consequences-and-Prevention/pretermbirth.ashx.

[36]   Race refers to mother's race.

[37]   Previously, a body mass index (BMI) at or above the 95th percentile of the sex-specific BMI growth charts was termed overweight. Beginning with *America's Children, 2010,* a BMI at or above the 95th percentile is termed obese to be consistent with other publications of National Health and Nutrition Examination Survey (NHANES) data. Estimates of obesity are comparable to estimates of overweight in past reports. Ogden, C.L., and Flegal, K.M. (2010) *Defining childhood obesity and overweight using body mass index (BMI).* National Health Statistics Report; Hyattsville, MD: National Center for Health Statistics. (forthcoming).

and to 17 percent by 2005–2006. In 2007–2008, 19 percent of children ages 6–17 were obese, not statistically different from the percentage in 2005–2006. Combined data for the years 2005–2008 indicate that Mexican American and Black, non-Hispanic children were more likely to be obese than White, non-Hispanic children.[38]

Poor eating patterns are a major factor in the high rate of obesity among children. In 2003–2004, on average, children's diets were out of balance, with too much added sugar and solid fat and not enough nutrient-dense foods, especially fruits, vegetables, and whole grains.[39] The average diet for all age groups met the standards for total grains, but only children ages 2–5 met the standards for total fruit and milk.

Depression can adversely affect the development and well-being of adolescents, and youth with a Major Depressive Episode (MDE) are at greater risk for suicide and initiation of substance use.[40] In 2008, 8 percent of adolescents ages 12–17 had at least one MDE during the past year. The prevalence of MDE was lowest in youth ages 12–13 (5 percent), compared with youth ages 14–15 (8 percent) and 16–17 (11 percent), and nearly three times higher among females (12 percent) compared with males (4 percent). The percentage of youth with at least one MDE receiving treatment for depression did not change significantly from 2004 to 2008 (40 percent and 38 percent, respectively).

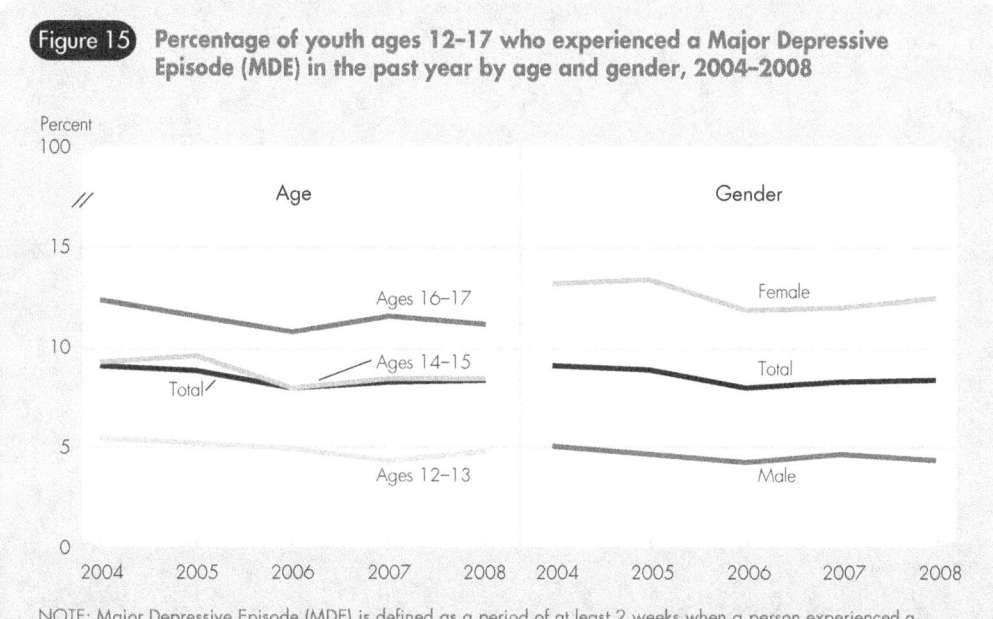

Figure 15 Percentage of youth ages 12–17 who experienced a Major Depressive Episode (MDE) in the past year by age and gender, 2004–2008

NOTE: Major Depressive Episode (MDE) is defined as a period of at least 2 weeks when a person experienced a depressed mood or loss of interest or pleasure in daily activities plus at least four additional symptoms of depression (such as problems with sleep, eating, energy, concentration and feelings of self-worth) as described in the 4th edition of the *Diagnostic and Statistical Manual of Mental Disorders (DSM-IV)*.

SOURCE: Substance Abuse and Mental Health Services Administration, National Survey on Drug Use and Health.

[38] National Center for Health Statistics, National Health and Nutrition Examination Survey (2010), unpublished tabulations. In this survey, respondents were asked to choose one or more races. All race groups discussed in this paragraph refer to people who indicated only one racial identity. Mexican American children may be of any race.

[39] The Healthy Eating Index-2005 measures how well diets meet the 2005 Dietary Guidelines for Americans. Guenther, P.M., Reedy, J., and Krebs-Smith, S.M. (2008). Development of the Healthy Eating Index-2005. *Journal of the American Dietetic Association, 108*(11): 1896–1901. U.S. Department of Health and Human Services and U.S. Department of Agriculture. (2005, January). *Dietary guidelines for Americans, 2005* (6th ed.). Washington, DC: U.S. Government Printing Office. Retrieved from http://www.health.gov/dietaryguidelines/dga2005/document/pdf/DGA2005.pdf.

[40] Shaffer, D., Gould, M.S., Fisher, P., Trautman, P., Moreau, D., Kleinman, M., and Flory, M. (1996). Psychiatric diagnosis in child and adolescent suicide. *Archives of General Psychiatry, 53*(4): 339–348. Substance Abuse and Mental Health Services Administration, Office of Applied Studies. (2007, May 3). *The NSDUH report: Depression and the initiation of cigarette, alcohol and other drug use among youths aged 12 to 17*. Rockville, MD: Author. Retrieved from http://oas.samhsa.gov/2k7/newUserdepression/newUserdepression.pdf.

America's Children at a Glance

	Previous Value (Year)	Most Recent Value (Year)	Change Between Years
Demographic Background			
Child population*			
Children ages 0–17 in the United States	74.4 million (2008)	74.5 million (2009)	↑
Children as a percentage of the population*			
Children ages 0–17 in the United States	24.5% (2008)	24.3% (2009)	↓
Racial and ethnic composition*			
Children ages 0–17 by race and Hispanic origin			
White	75.7% (2008)	75.6% (2009)	↓
White, non-Hispanic	55.9% (2008)	55.3% (2009)	↓
Black	15.2% (2008)	15.1% (2009)	↓
Asian	4.3% (2008)	4.4% (2009)	↑
All other races	4.7% (2008)	4.9% (2009)	↑
Hispanic (of any race)	21.9% (2008)	22.5% (2009)	↑
Family and Social Environment			
Family structure and children's living arrangements			
Children ages 0–17 living with two married parents	67% (2008)	67% (2009)	NS
Births to unmarried women			
Births to unmarried women ages 15–44	53 per 1,000 (2007)	52 per 1,000 (2008)	↓
All births that are to unmarried women	40% (2007)	41% (2008)	↑
Child care			
Children ages 0–4, with employed mothers, whose primary child care arrangement is with a relative	46% (2002)	48% (2005)	NS
Children ages 0–6, not yet in kindergarten, who received some form of nonparental child care on a regular basis	61% (2001)	61% (2005)	NS
Children of at least one foreign-born parent			
Children ages 0–17 living with at least one foreign-born parent	22% (2008)	22% (2009)	NS
Language spoken at home and difficulty speaking English			
Children ages 5–17 who speak a language other than English at home	21% (2007)	21% (2008)	NS
Children ages 5–17 who speak a language other than English at home and who have difficulty speaking English	5.2% (2007)	5.1% (2008)	↓
Adolescent births			
Births to females ages 15–17	22.2 per 1,000 (2007)	21.7 per 1,000 (2008)	↓
Child maltreatment			
Substantiated reports of maltreatment of children ages 0–17	11 per 1,000 (2007)	10 per 1,000 (2008)	↓

* Population estimates are not sample derived and therefore not subject to statistical testing. Change between years identifies differences in the proportionate size of these estimates as rounded. Percentages may not sum to 100 due to rounding.

America's Children in Brief: Key National Indicators of Well-Being, 2010

	Previous Value (Year)	Most Recent Value (Year)	Change Between Years
Economic Circumstances			
Child poverty and family income			
Related children ages 0–17 in poverty	18% (2007)	19% (2008)	↑
Secure parental employment			
Children ages 0–17 living with at least one parent employed year round, full time	77% (2007)	75% (2008)	↓
Food security			
Children ages 0–17 in households classified by USDA as "food insecure"	17% (2007)	22% (2008)	↑
Health Care			
Health insurance coverage			
Children ages 0–17 covered by health insurance at some time during the year	89% (2007)	90% (2008)	↑
Usual source of health care			
Children ages 0–17 with no usual source of health care	6% (2007)	6% (2008)	NS
Childhood immunization			
Children ages 19–35 months with the 4:3:1:3:3:1 combined series of vaccinations	77% (2007)	76% (2008)	NS
Oral health			
Children ages 5–17 with a dental visit in the past year	84% (2007)	84% (2008)	NS
Physical Environment and Safety			
Outdoor and indoor air quality			
Children ages 0–17 living in counties in which levels of one or more air pollutants were above allowable levels	65% (2007)	60% (2008)	NS
Drinking water quality			
Children served by community water systems that did not meet all applicable health-based drinking water standards	8% (2007)	6% (2008)	NS
Lead in the blood of children			
Children ages 1–5 with blood lead greater than or equal to 10 µg/dL	2% (1999–2002)	* (2005–2008)	NS
Housing problems			
Households with children ages 0–17 reporting shelter cost burden, crowding, and/or physically inadequate housing	40% (2005)	43% (2007)	↑
Youth victims of serious violent crimes			
Serious violent crime victimization of youth ages 12–17	10 per 1,000 (2007)	12 per 1,000 (2008)	NS
Child injury and mortality			
Injury deaths of children ages 1–4	13 per 100,000 (2005)	12 per 100,000 (2006)	NS
Injury deaths of children ages 5–14	8 per 100,000 (2005)	7 per 100,000 (2006)	↓
Adolescent injury and mortality			
Injury deaths of adolescents ages 15–19	50 per 100,000 (2005)	50 per 100,000 (2006)	NS

* Percentage is not shown because sample is too small to provide a statistically reliable estimate.

Legend NS = No statistically significant change   ↑ = Statistically significant increase   ↓ = Statistically significant decrease

	Previous Value (Year)	Most Recent Value (Year)	Change Between Years
Behavior			
Regular cigarette smoking			
Students who reported smoking daily in the past 30 days			
8th grade	3% (2008)	3% (2009)	NS
10th grade	* (2008)	6% (2009)	NS
12th grade	11% (2008)	11% (2009)	NS
Alcohol use			
Students who reported having five or more alcoholic beverages in a row in the past 2 weeks			
8th grade	8% (2008)	8% (2009)	NS
10th grade	* (2008)	18% (2009)	NS
12th grade	25% (2008)	25% (2009)	NS
Illicit drug use			
Students who reported using illicit drugs in the past 30 days			
8th grade	8% (2008)	8% (2009)	NS
10th grade	* (2008)	18% (2009)	NS
12th grade	22% (2008)	23% (2009)	NS
Sexual activity			
High school students who reported ever having had sexual intercourse	47% (2005)	48% (2007)	NS
Youth perpetrators of serious violent crimes			
Youth offenders ages 12–17 involved in serious violent crimes	11 per 1,000 (2007)	14 per 1,000 (2008)	NS
Education			
Family reading to young children			
Children ages 3–5 who were read to every day in the last week by a family member	60% (2005)	55% (2007)	↓
Mathematics and reading achievement			
Average mathematics scale score of			
4th-graders (0–500 scale)	240 (2007)	240 (2009)	NS
8th-graders (0–500 scale)	281 (2007)	283 (2009)	↑
Average reading scale score of			
4th-graders (0–500 scale)	221 (2007)	221 (2009)	NS
8th-graders (0–500 scale)	263 (2007)	264 (2009)	↑
12th-graders (0–500 scale)	287 (2002)	286 (2005)	NS

* Percentage is not shown because it is considered to be unreliable due to sampling error.

Legend   NS = No statistically significant change   ↑ = Statistically significant increase   ↓ = Statistically significant decrease

	Previous Value (Year)	Most Recent Value (Year)	Change Between Years
Education—continued			
High school academic coursetaking			
High school graduates who completed advanced coursework in			
Mathematics	45% (2000)	49% (2005)	↑
Science	63% (2000)	63% (2005)	NS
English	34% (2000)	31% (2005)	NS
Foreign language	30% (2000)	33% (2005)	↑
High school completion			
Young adults ages 18–24 who have completed high school	89% (2007)	90% (2008)	↑
Youth neither enrolled in school* nor working			
Youth ages 16–19 who are neither enrolled in school nor working	8% (2008)	9% (2009)	↑
College enrollment			
Recent high school completers enrolled in college the October immediately after completing high school	67% (2007)	69% (2008)	NS
Health			
Preterm birth and low birthweight			
Infants less than 37 completed weeks of gestation at birth	12.7% (2007)	12.3% (2008)	↓
Infants weighing less than 5 lb. 8 oz. at birth	8.2% (2007)	8.2% (2008)	NS
Infant mortality			
Deaths before first birthday	6.9 per 1,000 (2005)	6.7 per 1,000 (2006)	↓
Emotional and behavioral difficulties			
Children ages 4–17 reported by a parent to have serious difficulties with emotions, concentration, behavior, or getting along with other people	5% (2007)	5% (2008)	NS
Adolescent depression			
Youth ages 12–17 with past year Major Depressive Episode	8% (2007)	8% (2008)	NS
Activity limitation			
Children ages 5–17 with activity limitation resulting from one or more chronic health conditions	8% (2007)	9% (2008)	NS
Diet quality			
Average diet scores for children ages 2–17	Summary statistics excluded due to lack of comparability of data across the previous and most recent years. Please refer to http://childstats.gov/americaschildren/health6.asp.		
Obesity			
Children ages 6–17 who are obese	17% (2005–2006)	19% (2007–2008)	NS
Asthma			
Children ages 0–17 who currently have asthma	9% (2007)	9% (2008)	NS

* School refers to high school and college.

Legend   NS = No statistically significant change ↑ = Statistically significant increase ↓ = Statistically significant decrease

For further information, visit http://childstats.gov.   21

Recommended citation:

Federal Interagency Forum on Child and Family Statistics. *America's Children in Brief: Key National Indicators of Well-Being, 2010.* Washington, DC: U.S. Government Printing Office.

This report was printed by the U.S. Government Printing Office in cooperation with the National Center for Health Statistics, July 2010.

Single copies are available through the Health Resources and Services Administration Information Center while supplies last:
P.O. Box 2910
Merrifield, VA 22116

Toll-Free Lines:
1-888-Ask-HRSA
TTY: 1-877-4TY-HRSA

Fax: 703-821-2098
E-mail: ask@hrsa.gov

This report is also available on the World Wide Web:
http://childstats.gov

Federal Interagency Forum on Child and Family Statistics

The Federal Interagency Forum on Child and Family Statistics was founded in 1994. Executive Order No. 13045 formally established the Forum in April 1997 to foster coordination and collaboration in the collection and reporting of Federal data on children and families. Agencies that are members of the Forum as of Spring 2010 are listed below.

Department of Agriculture

Economic Research Service
http://www.ers.usda.gov

Department of Commerce

U.S. Census Bureau
http://www.census.gov

Department of Defense

Office of the Deputy Under Secretary of Defense, Military Community and Family Policy
http://prhome.defense.gov/mcfp

Department of Education

National Center for Education Statistics
http://nces.ed.gov

Department of Health and Human Services

Administration for Children and Families
http://www.acf.hhs.gov

Agency for Healthcare Research and Quality
http://www.ahrq.gov

Eunice Kennedy Shriver National Institute of Child Health and Human Development
http://www.nichd.nih.gov

Maternal and Child Health Bureau
http://www.mchb.hrsa.gov

National Center for Health Statistics
http://www.cdc.gov/nchs

National Institute of Mental Health
http://www.nimh.nih.gov

Office of the Assistant Secretary for Planning and Evaluation
http://aspe.hhs.gov

Substance Abuse and Mental Health Services Administration
http://www.samhsa.gov

Department of Housing and Urban Development

Office of Policy Development and Research
http://www.huduser.org

Department of Justice

Bureau of Justice Statistics
http://bjs.ojp.usdoj.gov

National Institute of Justice
http://www.ojp.usdoj.gov/nij

Office of Juvenile Justice and Delinquency Prevention
http://www.ojjdp.ncjrs.gov

Department of Labor

Bureau of Labor Statistics
http://www.bls.gov

Women's Bureau
http://www.dol.gov/wb

Department of Transportation

National Highway Traffic Safety Administration
http://www.nhtsa.dot.gov

Environmental Protection Agency

Office of Children's Health Protection
http://www.epa.gov/children/

National Science Foundation

Division of Science Resources Statistics
http://www.nsf.gov/statistics

Office of Management and Budget

Statistical and Science Policy Office
http://www.whitehouse.gov/omb/inforeg_statpolicy